ALONG THE WAY

by
Robert Wayne Clark

Robert Wayne Clark

DORRANCE & COMPANY
Philadelphia

Copyright © 1974 by Robert Wayne Clark
All Rights Reserved
ISBN 0-8059-2053-6
Library of Congress Catalog Card Number: 74-82215
Printed in the United States of America

In loving tribute
To my wife,
Who always made me feel
That I was better
Than I was;
Whose warm, assuring presence
Turned each bitter defeat
Into a shining victory;
And who built for herself
A life,
Fruitful and beautiful,
By pouring affection
And devotion
Into mine.

CONTENTS

Page

Today	1
On the Passing of a Poet	2
Horizons Unlimited	3
A Man Belovéd	4
Too Many Little Things We Leave Unsaid	5
Prayer for Brotherhood	7
To a Departed Secretary	8
Now You Know	9
Morning Prayer	10
Grace	11
Graduation	12
Let Me Be Me	14
I Shall Not Mind	15
Build On	17
Why	18
On Birthdays	20
Lines Written to a Recently Bereft Widow	21
When I Retire	22
The Burning Bush	24
I Wish I Were a Daffodil	25
Trail Blazers	26
It's Good, My Dear	27
Music	28
Take Comfort	29
I Am a United States Treasury War Bond	30
When I Was Three	33
You	34
I May Not Know	35

Requiem	37
A School	38
A Tiny Impulse	39
I Count Him Leader	40
Memory	41
To a Valiant Colleen	42
I Saw Stark Courage	43
The Voice of My America	44
Valentine for My Wife	45
I Love to be Alive	46
I Am America	47
He Also Served	49
Water	50
Garnering	52
The Worth of Life	54
Victory	55
Fishing	56
I Am a Layman	57
I Cry for My Son	59
Solicitude	61
Heritage	63
Tribute to a Beloved Leader	64

*To every mariner who sings
And sets his course toward better things:
God let you see with eye more clear
The star by which you choose to steer
And give your sailboat wings!*

TODAY

Today is my day,
Stretching its golden filament
Between the promise of a bright new dawn
And warm fulfillment at the eventide,
And bearing the hours it brings
Like jewels incomparable.

Today is my day
To weave into the pattern of my living
As I will:
Mine to choose
If I shall lavish all the patience,
Care,
And skill that I command
On this day's weaving;
Mine to choose
If I shall sit with idle hands and mind
To watch its strand unravel through its length
And strew its freight of precious pearls
Unheeded at my feet.

When dawn shall beckon me again,
Today will join the changeless train of yesterdays
That march their varied themes
Across the tapestry
I daily weave.

God give me wisdom
To look upward for the perfect pattern
As I weave,
And use this single, priceless day
That now is mine
While it is yet today.

ON THE PASSING OF A POET
(*Leigh Mitchell Hodges*)

Oh, Optimist, who goes as all men must
To rest in solemn hush eternally,
Whose husk in stern embrace returns to dust
And stills the vibrant voice that sang to me,
Fare on thy way, thy spirit full content
That shed its beauty lavishly that men
Might rise in courage though their strength was spent
And fill this anxious world with song again.
Rest on thy couch, thy endless slumber wooed
By melodies thy lyric heart first knew,
Thy robe a web of mankind's hopes renewed,
Thy requiem our stricken, mute adieu.
   Rest, Gentle Optimist, nor hear us weep;
   Each lilting cadence bring thee blessed sleep.

HORIZONS UNLIMITED

With every thought I read or hear,
   With every friend I find,
New roads across my world appear
   And beckon to my mind.

My world grows wider day by day,
   More filled with things to do;
And as it grows, in some strange way,
   I find I'm growing, too!

My eyes grow keener as I look
   Down long, broad avenues
That lead from almost any book
   I happen to peruse.

My steps grow firmer as I climb
   Each new, inviting crest;
My hands gain strength each added time
   They give a task their best.

I climb, and as my world's far rim
   Slips up against the sky,
I see its silver distance brim
   With new things I should try.

I'm sure I can't expect to go
   To where the earth and sky
Are crimped together like the dough
   That's crimped around a pie.

And so I'll see the world I know
   Grow bigger every dawn;
And as its edges stretch and grow,
   I'll keep on keeping on.

A MAN BELOVÉD
(*William H. Duncan*)

A man belovéd reaches forth and grows
   Beyond the human form that mortal eye
   Can see. And as the seasons hurry by,
His spirit, like the sun that comes and goes
But still is constant, ever outward flows.
   He is as one with all the lives that lie
   Like planets held against his tiny sky
Reflecting light and warmth his love bestows.

And if his pathway has been pre-designed
   To climb the sloping distance, it is well
To let him go. Then all who love will find
   That what is gone is but the empty shell
Whence flowed the noble impulse and the kind
   To choose their willing lives in which to dwell.

TOO MANY LITTLE THINGS WE LEAVE UNSAID

Too many little things we leave unsaid
That souls grow in nobility
And thrive upon.

We daily build
Each one
A warm, familiar world
Of tiny, fragile words;
Of words light-lipped
That seem to touch the flow and current of our lives
As petals brush the idlest ripple
Of a mighty stream.

When understanding,
Full and deep,
Has cradled warm affection in our hearts,
We glow,
And glory that these groping tendrils
Of our hurried lives
Can intertwine
To from a thing so precious.
Yet too soon
We learn to wear the wonder
At this miracle of intermingling lives
Like a worn and easy garment,
While the little words from which it grew
Wither like buds unopened
On our careless lips.

Too many flowers we strew
Above the senseless dust
To still our yearning for one last, short hour
To say the little things
We left unsaid—

The trifling words
That bloom, themselves,
We learn at tardy last,
Like fair and fragrant flowers
Above the roots that reach and search
Until they tap
The innermost recesses
Of our souls.

PRAYER FOR BROTHERHOOD

Lord, touch our hearts and make us blind
   To alien way, or tongue, or face,
And help us, loving all mankind,
   Build brotherhood in our small place.

And touch our unbeholding eyes
   That by Thy grace we come to see
The dull, drab world that round us lies
   Transformed as Thou wouldst have it be.

These tasks Thou setst before us, Lord,
   Bless to our spirits' strength and good;
And send us forth with one accord
   To labor in Thy neighborhood.

TO A DEPARTED SECRETARY
(*Clara Roberts Haas*)

With gracious purpose to our world she brought
   Her nimble fingers and her nimbler mind
   For service eager. In her nature kind
For stumbling feet on rocky steep she sought
Ascent more gentle. Miracles she wrought:
   Divining shafts of reason half-designed,—
   In wisdom waiting,—winnowing to find
A trump to wake to life our slumbering thought.

No martial leader she, whose brazen quests
   Are told in blighted life and graven stone;
No bold polemicist, whose honor rests
   On shattered idol and on tottered throne;
Our friend, our helper she, whose glory crests
   In poignant grief that we must walk alone.

NOW YOU KNOW

One thing divides go-getters
   From the boys who mope and moan,
And it's not athletic letters—
   It's backbone!

Just one thing takes a winner
   To the top of any hill;
And, for either saint or sinner,
   It's his will!

One measure only life employs
   To test if you are fit,
To separate the men and boys,
   And that's grit!

Nobody cares much where you've been,
   Or how your brain cells perk,
Or what's the color of your skin,
   If you work!

One quality you cannot stop
   With if's or and's or but's—
It takes you to the very top—
   And that's guts!

So if sometimes you've wondered why
   The things you try won't go,
Why all your planning goes awry,
   Now you know!

MORNING PRAYER

Lord, let me see against life's waking dawn
   The golden likeness of Thy purpose set;
And till the light shall fade and time be gone,
   Let not my heart forget.

Lord, let each thought I think, each deed I do
   Pour forth like pure and precious molten gold
To shape itself, for all mankind to view,
   Within Thy purposed mold.

When slanted rays shall tell me day is through,
   And from my soul the mortal husk is shorn,
Lord, let Thy purpose stand revealed anew
   As morning is reborn.

GRACE

As we surround this friendly board,
We ask Thy blessing on us, Lord:
Some little grace to see us through
This task that we together do;
Some gentleness and homey tact
To touch with sympathy each act;
And with it all a set of mind
To make us firmly just yet kind.
All this we ask that we may be
Fit representatives of Thee.
                          Amen

GRADUATION

These are our children
Who, brief days ago,
Slipped quietly into our waiting laps
And nestled there
Content
To woo their tinseled dreams
With chubby cheek
And tousled head
Against our happy hearts.

These are our children,
Yours and ours,
Who clambered through the spring
Of growing up.
Like things untamed
Which trail the rustic fence
Unmindful of its sure and rugged strength,
They leaned unknowing
On our willing love.
And when the sudden storm of childish woe
Broke briefly through their laughter,
They had but to touch their hurts
Against our faith
To romp away
Restored and whole
Again.

These are our children:
All our hopes,
Our prayers,
Our dreams of things to be
Wrought well and patiently
Into the living tissue of their souls.
Tonight they move

In awkward dignity
And fledgling pride
Across their little hour;
But when tomorrow comes,
The world is theirs.

God give us patience,
You and me,
To guide their rash, uncertain course
With kind restraint.
And give us faith
To see beyond the stumbling step,
The groping hand,
To see beyond the wayward gesture
Or the trifling heart,
And there behold with them
Their shining purpose
Arched across the flaming east.
Give us the courage
To relax the stern, restraining hand
That binds tomorrow close to yesterday,
And let these children
Open to our timid souls
A better world
Than we who plod the drabness
Of our middle years
Have ever dared to dream.

LET ME BE ME

Let me be me:
Through sweep of time and space
God dreamed this plan and hue of form and face
That little men conceive as alien race.
Let me be me.

Let me be me:
Grant my ancestral seed
The path to God that satisfied its need
Though little men call unknown pathways creed.
Let me be me.

Let me be me:
Though son of foreign land.
Where lies the virtue, let me understand,
That small men do by chance what I have planned?
Let me be me.

Let me be me:
Let me be free to find
Whatever glows like treasure to my mind
Though little men opine that I am blind.
Let me be me.

Let me be me:
And judge me by my will
To clasp the hands of all mankind until
The harsh discords of little men are still.
Let me be me.

I SHALL NOT MIND
(*1942*)

I shall not mind, nurse. Let me smile and know
That through some hero's veins this blood shall flow
Straight from my heart to his.
Let me feel
That from the greedy earth,
Harried by splintered steel
And drenched with scarlet sacrifice,
Some twisted stripling rises to rebirth,
Some youth whose faith is stronger than his fear
Is born anew to share my life.

Let me be near
As heavy, lifeless lids
Lift with the strength of this, my niggard gift,
And let me hear
The sobbing breath grow regular
And deep;
And let me watch a hero fall asleep.

I shall not mind, nurse. Let me follow on
Through tortured night
And screaming, fevered dawn
This boy who now is really part of me—
Blood of my blood—
Let me go on and see
A stormless tide,
A pleasant countryside,
A stoop worn smooth and splashed with friendly sun,
A graveled path with ivy overrun,
A door ajar to catch the stirring air,
A mother in her patient, endless round
Of tender, little duties
Taken unaware

By a familiar sound—
The joyous rush and crush of strong, young arms—
His arms—
And mine.

And let me share
With those who love and serve
This land of mine
And keep it free and clean
The glories of ten thousand dewy dawns
And gold-flecked sunsets
And the bursting joys that throng the hours between.

I shall not mind, nurse.
Mine is a coward soul
Cast in a narrow, unheroic mold.
Mine is a sheltered life, a drab, prosaic role.
I shall not mind, nurse.
Though I wince in fancied pain,
Open the vein
And from it let warm life unfold
For just one stricken boy again—
Open the vein!
Let my blood flow beyond this petty world
Through which I plod,
And let me be this fleeting once
This tiny bit
Like God.

BUILD ON

Build deep—
Secure within the rock the life you build
To stand unmoved when earth's last storms are stilled
That o'er you unabating, unrelenting sweep.
Build deep!

Build strong—
Let each succeeding deed, each guiding thought
Be planned in courage and in courage wrought
That strength flow through your life like cadenced song.
Build strong!

Build high—
Build from the lowly earth your loftiest dream
And from the topmost casement catch the gleam
That lifts the earth and life atop the sky.
Build high!

Build true—
Nor let your life's high-arching vault
Know from your hand one single, fleeting fault
To mar its silhouette against the blue.
Build true!

Build on—
The building of your life is never done:
Each finished task, a greater but begun;
Each crowded day, too soon forever gone.
Build on!

WHY

I cannot know the reason why,
Dear God,
The stately lily,
Perfumed rose,
Forget-me-not,
All lift their radiant faces,
Varihued,
To gaze upon the sun.
But this I know,
That in my garden
Where they spread their roots
Upon the bosom
Of the selfsame earth,
They lift their heads
Together
In a pattern
Far more beautiful to see
Than any one could hope to be
Alone.

Nor can I know,
God,
Why my skin is white
While all about me
Brothers,
Sons of Thine,
Lift countenances,
Varihued,
To read Thy will.

Condemn me not
To narrow, selfish pride
In what I did not do
Or could not help.

But rather let this heart
That beats within my breast
Have nobler vision
Than these erring eyes—
And let my soul behold,
As from the breathless height
Toward which we toil,
These sons of Thine
In common purpose joined
Like flowers in my garden,
Fairer far together
Than the fairest of them all
Could hope to be
Alone.

ON BIRTHDAYS

When I was as young as a wet-nosed kid,
I made an adventure of all I did.
Each day was as new as its sparkling morn
And I savored its hours like a child newborn.
Birthdays crept on reluctant feet,
And it seemed forever before we'd meet!

Now my chest has dropped; my hair has, too;
And arthritis comes with the morning dew;
And no matter how much delay I seek,
My birthdays crowd like the days of the week!
But greetings are lovely and friendship sweet;
So here in the homestretch I drag my feet!

LINES WRITTEN TO A RECENTLY BEREFT WIDOW

I cannot choose the moment
When my feet must cross the threshold
Leading forth from this brief time-locked bourne
In which we dwell.
I may not turn to wave goodbye—
As if my mind were busy somewhere else—
I may not stoop to kiss the lips I love the most,
Or pause one breathless second
Underneath the gentle pressure
Of the hands whose touch
Has made my whole life warm.
But if I seem to hasten thoughtlessly
From this, our little world
Whose slow-unfurling pageant has been beautiful
Because we were together,
I hasten not to leave these precious things we share
Because they pall upon me;
But instead I go
Because I hear my call.

And you will know
Within that loyal heart of yours
That through the years
Until at last your feet shall tread
The voiceless gate,
I'll know no greater joy
Than standing just inside
To wait for you.

WHEN I RETIRE

Don't let me count the years
Or turn again
With wistful eyes
To scan the cool and misty dawn
Where rose in brilliant gold
My youthful sun
And cast his light in dazzling wonder
On the fresh new world.

Don't let me count the years
Or turn again
Bold eyes of conquest
On the fruited noon
Where ruled in single glory
And in brazen radiance
The sun of my success
Deep-freighted
With the joy of doing
And of causing to be done
The all-engrossing business
Of a life lived fully
And with sharp intent.

Don't let me count the years
Or turn again
From this, the coppered splendor
Of my sun,
Which hangs against the hazy shades of eve
Poised like a patient monarch
Till the train of eager stars
That wait beyond the curtain of the years
Shall marshal

Him and all the things he means
Beyond the blessed edges
Of enfolding night.

Don't let me count the years
In meaningless rotation,
Crowded though they be
With memories
That flood the whirring wheel
To surfeit.
Let me rather loom from these,
The fragrant strands that mem'ry spins,
A pleasant coverlet
Of comfort and of deep content;
And let me lie the couch
My final years must know
And draw these glowing draperies
About my being
As I let my soul
In happy revel
Live and love and dream again
The days its joys reflect.

THE BURNING BUSH

"The bush burned with fire, and the bush was not consumed.... God called unto him out of the midst of the bush, and said, Moses, Moses. And he said, Here am I."—Exodus 3:2-4

In velvet hush of star-hung night,
   On breast of beating storm,
In fevered noontime's dazzling light,
   In twilight soft and warm,—
Through every zone and every clime,
So long as there be space and time,
The burning bush will ever be
For him whose spirit dares to see.

While, quavering, each timid soul
   That almost dares to see
The glory of the leader's role
   Shall, falt'ring, ask, "Why me?"
Through every zone and every clime,
So long as there be space and time,
The soul courageous makes reply,
"I see. I hear. Lord, here am I."

Once-fumbling hands with skill endowed,
   Once-sightless eyes that see,
Once-wayward feet, now sure and proud,
   Once-fettered souls, now free,—
Through every zone and every clime,
So long as there be space and time,
Will in numbered hordes rejoice
That someone heeded bush and voice.

I WISH I WERE A DAFFODIL

When April showers vale and hill,
I wish I were a daffodil:
In slender gown of new-washed green
I'd posture through the springtime scene.
I'd pirouette on tippy toe
In every breeze that chanced to blow.
I'd lift my golden cup and crown
High, where the biggest drops splashed down;
And when the playful shower was done,
I'd tilt my cup to catch the sun.
And when the chaliced tulips came
To touch the waking year with flame,
I'd drain my cup, I'd doff my gown,
Deep in the earth I'd snuggle down,
And there I'd dream of warm, soft rain
Till April happened by again.

TRAIL BLAZERS

But yesterday the road we striplings stride
   With confidence wound up the bitter slope
   In tortured mocking of ambitious hope
That dared to dream of heights its toil denied.
But yesterday bold giants, side by side,
   In valiant effort—nothing less—content,
   Attacked each frowning crag, each steep ascent,
And smoothed the way for him who truly tried.

Let them who so bestrode our narrow place
   And lifted with their love our tired eyes
     Be with us still our courage to inspire.
Let us behold the well-belovéd face
   Of each of these—the patient, kind and wise—
     Who touched our straining lives with sacred fire.

IT'S GOOD, MY DEAR

It's good, my dear,
To be a while apart—
To let the little ripples of remembering
Lap gently at the edges of my heart.

It's good, my dear,
For each of us to know
That through the youthful fire's complacent embering
The flame that warms us both is still aglow.

It's good, my dear,
To feel each empty mile
That drags its mocking length behind my wandering
Dissolving in the mem'ry of your smile.

It's good, my dear,
For each of us to see,
Whatever be the port of my meandering,
I'll always be with you and you with me.

MUSIC

Music is the first robin of spring
Tossing his heart to the April breeze.
It is the tiny brook stumbling over its pebbly bed,
And the breathless hush of a tranquil summer evening.
Music is the surging surf along the illimitable ocean
Hissing upon the insensible sands.
It is the chill wind of autumn
Gently stirring the dying leaves in early dawn,
And the soundless whisper of drifting snowflakes.

Music is the ecstatic thrill
Of young love just a-borning.
It is the warm, gurgling joy of an infant
And the comforting murmur of mother's voice
As she soothes the fancied injury of childhood.
It is the first halting recital of the six-year-old,
The glib and brash boastings of youth,
And the trembling tones of reminiscent old age.

Music is the strong, resonant voice of God's man
As he exhorts the laggards to holiness.
It is the brazen blast of martial trumpets
Glorifying conflict.
Music is love and hate,
Enmity and brotherhood;
It is joyous laughter,
And throttled silence,
And deep, unbearable grief.

Music is all the sound
And all the stillness
Of life.

TAKE COMFORT

Take comfort
That the Master Weaver chose
A strand so fine of texture
And so delicate of hue
To lie across life's pattern
With your own.

Take comfort
That no solitary strand
Can lie in single beauty:
That the blue is bluer still
Against the shining gold—
In turn more radiant.

Take comfort
That the web and the design of life
Are loomed in endless purpose;
That each finished skein
Adds strength and glory
By its having been
To all that follows.

Take comfort.

I AM A UNITED STATES TREASURY WAR BOND
(*1943*)

I am a United States Treasury War Bond.
I am just one unnecessary day,
Or hour, or minute
Of war.
I am a new, useless Tarawa,
A wanton Salerno.
I am the sudden impact of wingéd death,
The reddening mist, the eternal black and the silence.
I am the reeling pitch of the stricken ship,
The bitter stinging salt and strangling agony
And merciful end of everything.
I am the shrieking, plunging inferno
And the quick compassionate veil of dark
That shrouds the pilot.
I am the swirl of oily waters that grows calm and is lost
In the pathless expanse of ocean.

I am a United States Treasury War Bond.
I am the men and the women
Who wouldn't have needed to go.
I am the tears
And the stifling anguish of parting;
I am the courage and the stern, cold anger
And the inflexible will of free men and women.
I am the waiting—
The suspense—the long silence—
And the waiting.
I am the bitter impotent tears of the bereft;
The hot, dry eyes, the beaten hopes, the desolated lives;
The quiet grieving and the acquiescent prayers of those
Whose full years blend tranquilly with the forever.
I am the deserted streets,
The books unwritten and the songs unsung;

The temple of the new day still unplanned,
Its stones unquarried,
And its bell forever voiceless.

I am a United States Treasury War Bond.
I am the peace that might have come one day,
Or hour, or minute
Sooner.
I am the chubby arms, the soft, warm cheek,
And the shrill, delighted welcome of little children.
I am the eager, dusty forepaws
Against the khaki tunic, and the shaggy head
Nuzzling happily the familiar hand.
I am the calm, the deep, the restful love of women,
The ache of waiting past,
The glad release that kindles lips and eyes.
I am the quick, hard pressure of the hand,
The studied casual word and mien
That speaks a man's affection.
I am the first love of youth—
The perfume of the waking world,
The unspoken word and the tender caress.
I am the numbed and lifeless hearts,
The empty arms,
The lonesome journey and the unfinished dream.
I am the grateful mellowing memory of each voice
That speaks no more.

I am a United States Treasury War Bond.
I am the challenge to America:
I am the blood of America's youth,
The genius of America's new generation,
Her hope of a glorious dawn
Arising from this shattered night.
I am the powerful shoulders, the head held high,
The deep-throated contentment,

And the confident stride across freshly furrowed acres.
I am the serenity of America's mothers;
The faith of America's children;
The calm security of America's age.
I am the blue star that need never turn to gold.
I am the challenge of America's progress,
Of her great heroes
And her lesser heroes who followed them
And will follow them again,
To victory.

I am a United States Treasury War Bond.

WHEN I WAS THREE

When I was three,
  I could not see
    Beyond each rising of the sun;
It seemed to me
  All time must be
    Just like the day but new-begun.

But since I've grown,
  I'm glad to own
    I see beyond today and know
That meadows sown
  With blooms full-blown
    Lie sleeping under winter's snow.

YOU

From here your path through the world appears
  As smooth as the lilt of a song;
But wherever you go down the trail of years,
  You'll have to take YOU along.

Your path may circle this shrinking globe,
  Or blaze through its limitless blue;
To the smothered depths of earth you may probe,
  But you cannot escape from YOU.

As you choose your books, you choose your friends
  From an endless and varied shelf;
But the beauty and strength of friendship depends
  On your getting along with YOUrself.

Approach every job with a ready hand
  And know in your heart it's true:
For whatever purpose your work is planned,
  You will always be building YOU.

When you're tempted to slight this YOU you build,
  Stop short for a long, clear view:
All the things with which your life is filled
  You must take along with YOU.

From here your path through the world appears
  As smooth as the lilt of a song.
Take love in your heart down that path of years
  And be glad to have YOU along.

I MAY NOT KNOW

I may not see
The face and form of God
Though I may turn my eyes
Upon the infinite miracle of space
Where float in haze of mystery
Uncounted worlds,
Though I may probe
With reverent eye and clear
The fragile miracle
Of one forget-me-not.

I may not hear
The voice of God
Though I may listen to all nature:
To the muted hush and chill
Of autumn's narrowing cell;
To lisping freshet
Tumbling headlong through the waking spring;
Or to the bold, majestic thunder
Wheeling out among the trembling stars.

I may not know
The will of God
Save as I sense
The gentle pressure of solicitude
Against my erring heart.

For God has given us
To will
And, having willed,
To act.

But as I grow,
I slowly climb the stubborn slope

Beyond whose crest
The edges of eternity lap gently.
And if I turn,
And let my vision trace—
Like slanted rays at sunset
Through the aureate haze—
The pattern I have wrought
By deeds I've done,
Words spoken,
Thoughts I've nurtured in my secret soul,
I'll know at last
How God has seemed to me
And in that moment
How my life has seemed
To God.

REQUIEM

When evening falls for me
   And God shall say,
"The days allotted thee
   Are flown away,"

Mourn not the lifeless clay
   Whence I shall flee:
Wander where children play—
   There will I be.

A SCHOOL

It isn't the building that's really the school,
  Nor the teachers long laboring in it;
It isn't the students who study or fool
  As they're moved by the whim of the minute.

It isn't the lessons, the themes or the sums,
  Or the playground in bright, sunny weather;
Or even the deep understanding that comes
  From living and working together.

But deep in the midst of all of these things,
  Where you must listen closely to hear it,
There's a something that pulses, and surges, and sings:
  It's a thing of the heart and the spirit.

It flows from its building, a limitless tide,
  Engulfing the whole world it reaches;
It floods through the souls of the folk far and wide,
  And builds in the heart what it teaches.

School buildings may crumble, and teachers depart
  But the school that is real will continue;
For a school is a thing of the spirit and heart:
  It isn't beside, it's within you.

A TINY IMPULSE

A tiny impulse
Sprang to life,
Warm-soft and dewy
As the truant droplets
From an April shower
That bead with silver pearls
The fresh, scarce-burgeoned leaflets
Of the waking willow.

A tiny impulse
Pressed against the unsuspecting tenor
Of an ordered life
As seeps a vagrant wisp
Of shower-washed zephyr,
Unperceived,
Between the bare and rigored boles
That guard the citadel.

A tiny impulse
Struck the years away,
The pleasant shackles
Habited upon a life content
To see its own reflection cast
Against the narrow mirror of its wont.

A tiny impulse
Sprang to brief, amorphous life
And from the tasteless dust
Of just another ordinary day
Pressed out one precious breath
Of rare perfume.

I COUNT HIM LEADER
(*Allen H. Wetter*)

I count him leader on whom I rely
   To point the road, then take it at my side,
   At once my fellow worker and my guide,
More boldly shouldered to the load than I.
I count him leader who, with cheerful eye,
   Appraises thought and effort I've applied
   To rear the structure of our common pride,
And owns the debt that lesser men deny.

I count him leader who is keen of mind,
   Upon whose simple word I can depend,
Who has the manly courage to be kind,
   Who has no skill to flatter or pretend;
And then, because I'm human, I'm inclined
   To count him leader who can count me friend.

MEMORY

With half-closed eyes upon your pillow lie
And let the beauty of the world drift by:
The scent of roses and the breath of spring,
The wheeling gull, the chipmunk's chattering,
The friendly smile, a baby's gurgling laugh,
The wobbling steps of newborn foal or calf,
The gold-tipped ripples on a summer stream,
The taste of apples and the feel of cream,
The smell of Christmas trees, a snowdrop's bloom,
The restful warmth of some familiar room.

With these and countless more our world is blessed;
Watch them go drifting by and take your rest
With grateful heart that what we sense or see
God lets us store up in our memory.

TO A VALIANT COLLEEN
(*Edith Hanna*)

This hand that wiped each streaming eye and nose,
  In hope that in the vacuum behind
  Might lurk some hint of slowly waking mind,
Gives up nor hope nor hanky at the close
Of dream-crammed years a valiant colleen chose
  To spend as mentor to the disinclined,
  The wayward, cusséd, and the unrefined
Whom on unwary parents God bestows.

This eye that sees the truth shine through deceit,
  This tongue that's touched with Erin's gentle fire,
This mind that counted compromise defeat,
  This voice that lifts its lash but to inspire,
This heart that cannot understand retreat—
  Who dares allege their owner could retire?

I SAW STARK COURAGE

I saw stark courage walk the streets today:
A wispy mother
Bosomless and thin
With making much too little seem enough.
One infant fist she clutched
With starveling hand;
A second infant clawed
In desperate stride
Her drab and faded garment;
Still another
Thrust his heels and buttocks
High against her weary heart
And swelled to bursting
With his lust for fuller life
Her niggard body.
This I saw
And then the touch of fire
That waked the somber blueness of her eyes
And lighted with the glow of high design
The gaunt expanse of empty cheek and brow;
I saw the tilted chin,
The sculpted contour of the lifted head,
And all the weight of petty cares I know
Dropped from my shoulders
As I stood abashed.

THE VOICE OF MY AMERICA

There is no voice of my America
Save as I lift
My single, slender voice
To give it strength and purpose.
There is no noble goal—
No high ideal—
Of my America
Save as, within my inmost heart,
I nourish it,
Save as its roots are anchored
In the thoughts and deeds
That are my living.

For I must understand
That I
Am all of my America
That I control,

And if
The voice of this, my native land,
Shall one day lift itself
In thund'rous challenge
Hurled across the rhythmic turbulence
That is our world,
And if
Mankind shall one day rise in bold response
To snatch the gauntlet
And to dare
The lowering foes athwart the spiraled path,
My single, slender voice
Will be the only one that I may lift
To swell the mighty chorus
Men will call
The voice of my America.

VALENTINE FOR MY WIFE

With what fresh thought, what deeply freighted word
   Does man describe a true and loyal wife,
Whose heart is his through tranquil hour or strife—
Through stroke sublime, discomfiture absurd;
Who sees her hopes in life ofttimes deferred;
   Who fills her hours with calm scarce-spoken dreams;
   Who lives not on what is but on what seems;
Nor lets one hint of mild complaint be heard?

This is the wife God's wisdom gave to me—
   A wife whose courage both of us has served;
Who lived her life as if what had to be
   Was always best for us; who never swerved
From pouring love and hope, forever free,
   To fill my life with sweetness undeserved.

I LOVE TO BE ALIVE

When May arrives, I wonder why
   I seem to love it so;
Its fragrant hours hurry by
   Almost before I know.

Then June is here; the apples bloom
   And bees buzz busily;
I stretch myself and find I've room
   To love June lustily.

July and August come along,
   September's smile is gay,
And still I find my lover's song
   Sincere as back in May.

And so it goes the whole year through
   Till May is back again,
Through winter's snow and summer's dew
   My heart sings love's refrain.

Perhaps I know the reason why
   The months as they arrive
Can claim my love: it may be I
   Just love to be alive.

I AM AMERICA

A soldier died—
His bold, young courage
Splashed in scarlet waste
Across some alien barren—
All the promise of deep-fruited plenty
Spent
In one consuming flash of sacrifice.
And what is that to me?

A mother's heart
Is wrenched at parting from a son
Still cradled in the womb
Of her affection.
A father,
Weighted low with grief
And weighted more with being brave himself
Stares with unseeing eyes
Against the dull, gray emptiness of days undawned.
And what is that to me?

Within my heart,
My mind,
That boy must live
And through my being
Reach the nurturing sun
To bring to full fruition all the promise
Of the life he gave.
I must build—
As surely he would build—
A pride
To soothe away a mother's anguish
And a father's speechless grief.

A hero's life,
The little things he loved,
The stars toward which he strove
Must intermingle with my own;
And I must build
Within my life
For all mankind to see
America,
The land he died to keep secure
And free.

HE ALSO SERVED
(*Leon J. Obermayer*)

To him in whom youth's need for knowing found
   A champion who crowded busy days
   To overflowing fullness finding ways
To set their feet with love on firmer ground—
To him, with fruitful years and many crowned,
   Let grateful hearts and grateful voices raise
   In chorused harmony our hymn of praise
Till through time's vaulted domes its echoes sound:

This is a man. He well knew how to weigh
   Each thought, each plan, each act as it deserved;
Unmoved by friends or critics' stern array,
   From course with courage set he never swerved;
He labored as his tribute to the day,
   And led us well because he also served.

WATER

Water—
Lighting as if with tiny diamonds
The dewy meadow
As the first rays of morning sun
Illuminate each droplet
To toss its multicolored brilliance
Against the happy, dazzled eyes
Of children.
Water.

Water—
Tripping as though alive
Above the shingle
In the mountain brooklet's bed;
Tossing its truant drops
Against the overhanging banks,
Then clipping back
To course the willowed channel
Fronting rocky faces
It has worn through countless years,
Then tumbling with a sheer abandoned joy
Into the bosom of the river.
Water.

Water—
Unbridled, angry, raging water
Sweeping aside in turbulent career
The warmth and comfort
Of the friendly home,
Man's sweet, beloved retreat
From each day's jousting
In a rushing world of fevered conflict.
Water.

Water—
Gathering into its terrible, insatiable maw
All the long-familiar handlings
Of the homely daily life
Of those who, unsuspecting, unoffending, cower
Before the drenching torrent of destructive might
That rides its cold, unwelcome coming.
Water.

Water—
That leaves man homeless,
Helpless,
And afraid;
That bids him roll the years away
And build anew a way of living
And a way of nurturing his loves.
Water.

Water—
That softly falls to earth
To nourish all that grows
And holds in God-like mien
The promise of a bounteous harvest.
Water.

GARNERING

This is my life
To do with as I will:
To fill to surfeit
With the gilded wealth of things—
To have and hold but not to share—
Till last these grasping hands,
In final agony of parting life,
Shall spread their talons
Like a palsied shadow of themselves
And rain the gathered worldly wealth
About my cold, unsensing feet
In empty, meaningless cascade;
While this, my coward soul,
Slinks back unsung,
Unmourned,
Among the shades of those whose lives
Are given to unholy garnering.

This is my life
To do with as I will:
To gather to itself in joyous plenty
From the multitude of yearning souls
Its being touches
A wealth untold of love,
Of blessing,
And of golden gratitude
That through the years
My hands have opened
Like the precious bloom of bounteous summer
To strew along the pathway I have trod
Some little good,
Some blesséd sharing
Of the bounty God has trusted to my keeping.
Wealth no hand can hold

Nor, yielding to the calm of earthly death,
No hand can lose.
Then I shall go
From this brief bourne of want and plenty
To blend my being blessed—
My garnered wealth—
Into the boundless tide of blessing
That shall wash the shores
Of that eternal sea
To which I, joyous,
Shall at last return.

THE WORTH OF LIFE

The worth of life
Is never measured by the span of years
That God allots
However far their fabric draws itself
Or ornaments each golden strand
With gleaming days and hours.

The worth of life
Is rather measured by man's service
To mankind,
By countless little kindnesses,
Performed within the narrow boundaries
Where the truly helpful heart
Opening freely, pours itself in copious draught
Into the chalice of a thirsting soul.

So has it been with him
Who walked in kindly service
To the lives he knew,
And magnified the stature of his life
By giving precious days and hours
As he went
To serve his brothers.

This be our tribute
To this man we love:
That as he served,
He lived and walked among us
Bringing riches unimagined
To the lives of all
Who brushed, in passing by,
The towering greatness
Of a modest man.

VICTORY
(William Schermerhorn)

When untried youth life's mountain trail essayed,
  The steep ascent his stripling strength denied;
  Sharp crags and rugged turned his steps aside,
And mocking echoes keened the tortured grade.
Through lowered skies flashed lightning's brilliant blade,
  The clouds unloosed on earth a stifling tide
  That spurned with raw defeat each fledgling stride;
Then bitter blasts his bursting heart dismayed.

A man there was of lofty deed and thought,
  His hand extended with a will designed
To lift the youth to reach the goal he sought,
  His motive selfless and his impulse kind;
Together youth and man their purpose wrought:
  To reach the crest where victory's enshrined.

FISHING

When I was only half-past-three
And all the world was new to me,
I learned the beauty of the rain,
The sun that always beamed again,
The gray, the blue, the curdled sky,
The clouds that drooped or hurried by,
The joy of doing or just wishing,
Because my daddy took me fishing.

As years and seasons spiraled by
And life approached its own July,
It brought its trouble and its pain
That blotted out the sun and rain.
I joined life's pushing, grasping crowd
And seldom even saw a cloud;
All I could do was keep on wishing
That dad were here to take me fishing.

Perhaps before my life is flown
I'll have a youngster of my own
To teach about the joys I knew
When sun was gold and sky was blue,
When dad and I would gaily plod
Some riverbank with creel and rod.
Till then I know I'll keep on wishing
I had someone to take out fishing.

I AM A LAYMAN

I am a layman,
Uninitiate;
No sacred rite of ordination
Consecrates me,
Dedicates these hands,
These feet,
This heart and mind
To priestly office.
Mine is to hearken, to believe, obey,
And then to follow.

But I know
That if God walks
Among my fellowmen
Beyond the walls
That gird this sanctuary,
He must walk upon these layman's feet
Of mine.
And if God stoops
To lift a son,
Unworthier still than I,
To nobler living,
He must lift that son
With these,
My layman's hands.
And if God's blessing
Flows across the tiny world
Through which I plod,
To quick to virtuous life
The men whose lives I touch,
Then must that blessing flow
Through these,
My layman's mind and layman's heart.

I am a layman,
Uninitiate;
No sacred rite of ordination
Consecrates me,
Dedicates these hands,
These feet,
This heart and mind
To priestly office.
Yet the touch of God
Transforms me
So that I become
In truth
The single instrument
To work His will.

I CRY FOR MY SON

I cry for my son
Who in infancy crowed and gurgled
And wept himself into my heart;
Who grew slowly and beautifully
To vigorous manhood—
With a mind frail
And unequal to the task of governing his body.

I cry for my son:
I cry in the anguish of my motherhood
That I can lend him assistance
And support no more;
For I am powerless to plumb the depths
Of this, his mental need
And pour my love
Into the empty vessel of his thinking.

I cry for my son—
For help for my son—
For he has offended his neighbor
And mine.
Who knows the darkest caverns of the vagrant mind?
Who can dig deep into the tortuous labyrinths of thought?
Who can give the help
My love knows not how to give?
My God! Not the walls of numb, cold stone!
Not the brazen bars to shut the sun away!
Not man's forgetfulness and stark indifference!

I cry for my son.
Out of the womb I bore him,
Happy in careless childhood;

Let me endure the travail once again
To give my son a sturdy mind.

I cry for my son.

SOLICITUDE

Lord, let me hunger
With the humble, hungering horde
That Thou has brought
To people earth,
And gasp and choke with those who suffer thirst;
Let me know racking pain
With those who ail
And grope through murky pathways
With benighted sons
Who struggle in unlettered sightlessness.

Lord, let me, warm and tender,
Guard and guide to holiness
The innocence of childhood;
Let me reach out to the warmth
And temper with affection the coldness
Of these, my brothers, grown to adult state.
Let me trudge the toilsome highway
With the lame,
And the low, slow road
On which the uncomplaining agéd make their way.

Lord, let me cry
With brokenhearted sons of sorrow and of loneliness;
Let me leap no less in joy
With those who taste of gladness.
Let me clasp the hands of all Thy children,
Sad or joyful,
In perfect love and perfect sympathy.

Lord, let me act
To lift the feet of every son of Thine
Whom I may touch,
Nor yet by any action done or left undone

Bring pain to any man
Thy heart may know.
Let me with all the fullness of my strength
Cherish the noble purposes
Thy sons may treasure,
Nor injure one.

Lord, let me hear Thee speak
In every note
Of pleasant or discordant voice
My brother utters;
Let me lend an open and receptive ear
To hear the patient voice that is my teacher;
Let me do Thy will,
Simply and dutifully,
Because it is Thy will.

Lord, let me do these things
Without cessation or abatement,
All my life,
For I am sure that in their absence
Lies the greatest sin of man:
Complacency—
The sin of being satisfied, or even pleased,
With what is narrow, selfish and unblest:
With things I say,
With things I do,
With things I am.

HERITAGE

Oh, Man, who sprang from joyous mother's womb
   And frolicked through a childhood rapt and sweet,
   Who built a life of triumph and defeat
And seasoned it with happiness and gloom,
Your numbered days are counted. In the tomb
   You lay your weary form of life bereft;
   And those about you wonder: What is left
That greedy earth cannot in time consume?

Know this: The love you lavished as you strode
   The rugged path of life can never die;
The words you spoke that took their warm abode
   In lives a-shaping even death defy;
The pattern your life set cannot erode
   Nor time its usefulness to youth deny.

TRIBUTE TO A BELOVED LEADER
(Aleda E. Druding)

The lovely book is read,
Each page of wisdom gleaned
And gladness,
Each precious thought
Turned musingly upon the distaff of the mind
And spun into the fiber
Of unseeking service
To men's children.

The lovely book is read,
But with the final page
Such memories of the reading flood our hearts—
Of leadership undaunted,
Modest pride,
Of inspiration,
Help,
Companionship,
And through it all of quiet, calm concern
And warm affection—
Such memories of the reading flood our hearts
That while time turns its orbit
Through the miracle of ever-wheeling stars
The final cover never shall be closed.